46664

A Little, Brown Book

First published in Great Britain in 2004
by Little, Brown in association with 46664 and the Nelson Mandela Foundation

A CIP catalogue record for this book is available from the British Library.

ISBN 0 316 73017 3

Typeset in Stencil, Clarendon, Impact, Confidential, Egypto by Wherefore Art?

Manufactured in China by Imago

Little, Brown
An imprint of
Time Warner Book Group UK
Brettenham House
Lancaster Place
London WC2E 7EN

www.twbg.co.uk

46664

46664
CONCERTS

MOST PEOPLE TALK ABOUT 46664 AS A CONCERT THAT HAPPENED IN AFRICA SOMEWHERE, SOMETIME. WITH THE WORLD MOVING SO FAST NOW, TOO OFTEN AN EVENT SUCH AS THIS APPEARS AS A TINY BLIP IN SOME RADAR SOUP THAT IS GROANING WITH THE AMOUNT OF CYBER-INFORMATION BEING POURED INTO IT EVERY NANOSECOND.

AND JUST LIKE A BAD CHEF WHO PUTS TOO MANY INGREDIENTS INTO HIS EXCESSIVELY RICH MEAL, WE ARE ALL FEELING SLIGHTLY QUEASY FROM THE OVERLOAD OF INFORMATION BOUNCING OFF OUR RETINAS AND SHAKING OUR MALLEUS.

YET, AMONGST ALL THE SPAM AND MARKETING AND DUBIOUS NEWS SOUND BITES, EVERY NOW AND THEN THERE IS A SMALL PEBBLE OF NOURISHING CLARITY DROPPED INTO THIS SEA OF WORDS AND IMAGES THAT GETS OUR ATTENTION -- AND IN THIS CASE, IT IS HAS BEEN CAST BY NELSON MANDELA.

THIS IS NO ORDINARY STONE. THIS IS A STONE LIKE A KOMBOLOI BEAD THAT HAS BEEN WORN SMOOTH BY TWENTY-SEVEN YEARS OF GENTLE THOUGHT, MEDITATION AND INTENTION BEFORE BEING PITCHED INTO TODAY'S DEEP AND SHARK-INFESTED LACUNA.

I WAS SWIMMING JUST BELOW THE SURFACE OF THIS GREAT LACUNA WHEN I SAW A SMILING FACE LOOKING DOWN INTO THE WATER AND THROWING SOMETHING THAT LOOKED LIKE A STONE... SO I CAUGHT IT.

THIS TURNED OUT TO BE NOT A PEBBLE OR A STONE, BUT A NUMBER -- 46664 -- THAT A MAN HAD BEEN CARRYING AROUND FOR NEARLY FIVE DECADES.

46664... IS IT A MYSTERY CODE? IS IT A PLACE IN TIME? IS IT A PHONE NUMBER?

I RAN WITH THAT NUMBER AND WANTED TO TELL EVERYONE I KNEW WHAT IT WAS -- NELSON MANDELA'S PRISON NUMBER FROM HIS YEARS OF UNJUST INCARCERATION IN ROBBEN ISLAND FOR STANDING UP AGAINST APARTHEID IN SOUTH AFRICA.

46664 IS, AND WILL BE, ALL OF THESE OTHER THINGS I HAVE JUST MENTIONED FOR YEARS TO COME. FOR THE MOMENT, HOWEVER, IT IS ALSO A BRILLIANT PEBBLE MAKING RIPPLES THAT ARE TURNING INTO SMALL WAVES ON TOP OF AN OCEAN OF INDIFFERENCE.

WHEN I WAS TALKING TO MR.MANDELA ON THE TELEPHONE, I WAS EXCITEDLY TELLING HIM MY IDEAS ABOUT USING THE NUMBER AS A TELEPHONE NUMBER TO DIAL IN DONATIONS WHILE LISTENING TO EXCLUSIVE SONGS... OR USING IT AS A WEB ADDRESS FOR ONLINE DONATIONS, ETC.

THEN, HE SAID: "WELL. THE WORLD IS MOVING SO FAST WITH TECHNOLOGY, NOW YOU CAN TAKE CARE OF ALL THAT. BUT I REMEMBER WHEN, IN ORDER TO PASS A MESSAGE, I WOULD JUST STAND ON THE HILL AND SHOUT TO MY NEIGHBOUR 'HELLO MY FRIEND... HOW ARE YOU?' AND HE WOULD SHOUT BACK 'I'M FINE... HOW ARE YOU?'"

NOWADAYS, THERE IS SO MUCH NOISE TO COMPETE WITH AND WE NEED TO DROWN OUT THESE DISSONANT SOUNDS WITH ONES THAT ARE MELODIC AND HARMONIOUS.

SO, IN COLLABORATION WITH FRIENDS AND COLLEAGUES, WE ALL DECIDED TO HOLD A CONCERT -- TO MAKE A LOT OF BEAUTIFUL NOISE IN ORDER TO BE SEEN/HEARD FIRST... AND TO DROP THIS CONCERT, LIKE THE PEBBLE, INTO THE SUBCONCIOUS OF PEOPLE AROUND THE WORLD TO MAKE THE FIRST RIPPLES, BRINGING AIDS AWARENESS TO PEOPLE AND GOVERNMENTS AS AN ISSUE OF HUMAN RIGHTS AND UNDERSTANDING.

NOW THAT IT HAS BEEN DONE, THE WAVES ARE APPEARING ON MANY DISTANT SHORES AND WILL CONTINUE TO DO SO AS LONG AS I AND MANY OTHERS GO WITH THE CURRENT AND RIDE THE WAVES... BECAUSE, JUST LIKE WATER, TRUTH WILL FIND ITS WAY.

I WOULD PARTICULARLY LIKE TO THANK ROGER TAYLOR, BRIAN MAY, JIM BEACH , SIR RICHARD BRANSON, J. F. CECILLION, LIZZIE ANDERS (MUSIC MATRIX) AND JOHN M. SAMUEL (THE NELSON MANDELA FOUNDATION). THEY WERE ALL THERE AT THE BEGINNING AND ARE STILL ONGOING DRIVING FORCES FOR 46664.

I ALSO WANT TO THANK MY CLOSE FRIENDS BONO AND BOB GELDOF, WHO AS EXPERT HELMSMEN, SKILLFULLY AND SUCCESSFULLY STEERED THE COURSE.

AND LAST, BUT NOT LEAST, THANK MR.NELSON MANDELA HIMSELF FOR BEING SUCH AN INSPIRATION TO US ALL.

DAVE STEWART

46664 is a vital campaign to help fight a tragedy of unprecedented proportions which is claiming more lives than the sum total of all wars, famines and floods. Aids is no longer just a disease, it is a human rights issue. It affects people of all ages but in particular it affects young people. Young people in Africa. For the sake of all of them we must act and act now.

For the past six months my friends from the worlds of music, business, technology and entertainment have been discussing with the Nelson Mandela Foundation what more they can do. Together, the decision was taken to create 46664.

46664 was my prison number; for the eighteen years that I was imprisoned on Robben Island I was known as just a number. Millions of people today infected with Aids are just that - a number. They too are serving a prison sentence - for life. So I have allowed my prison number, 46664, to help drive this campaign.

46664 will work with governments, charities, artists and individuals around the world to lead the fight to rid Africa of HIV and to help those affected by Aids. It is a unique global initiative using the universal language of music, and the latest technology, to take our message to the greatest possible audience. This evening's concert features artists from all over the globe who are helping 46664 to reach our youth, so important to ensure that in future we can live in a world free from HIV and Aids.

But tonight is just the beginning of the campaign. It is the first of a number of events marking a long-term commitment by the Nelson Mandela Foundation and the sponsors and partners of 46664.com.

Together we can fight Aids and help secure a future for everyone.

I thank you. NELSON MANDELA

ARRIVAL

BUT IF EVERYONE MAKES A BIG DEAL ABOUT THIS CAUSE AND TAKES IT TO THEIR HEARTS THEN I THINK PEOPLE WILL REALISE THERE IS NO STIGMA ANY MORE. IT'S JUST SOMETHING THAT'S ATTACKING HUMANITY, AS NELSON MANDELA SAYS, AND WE HAVE TO FIGHT TOGETHER. **BRIAN MAY**

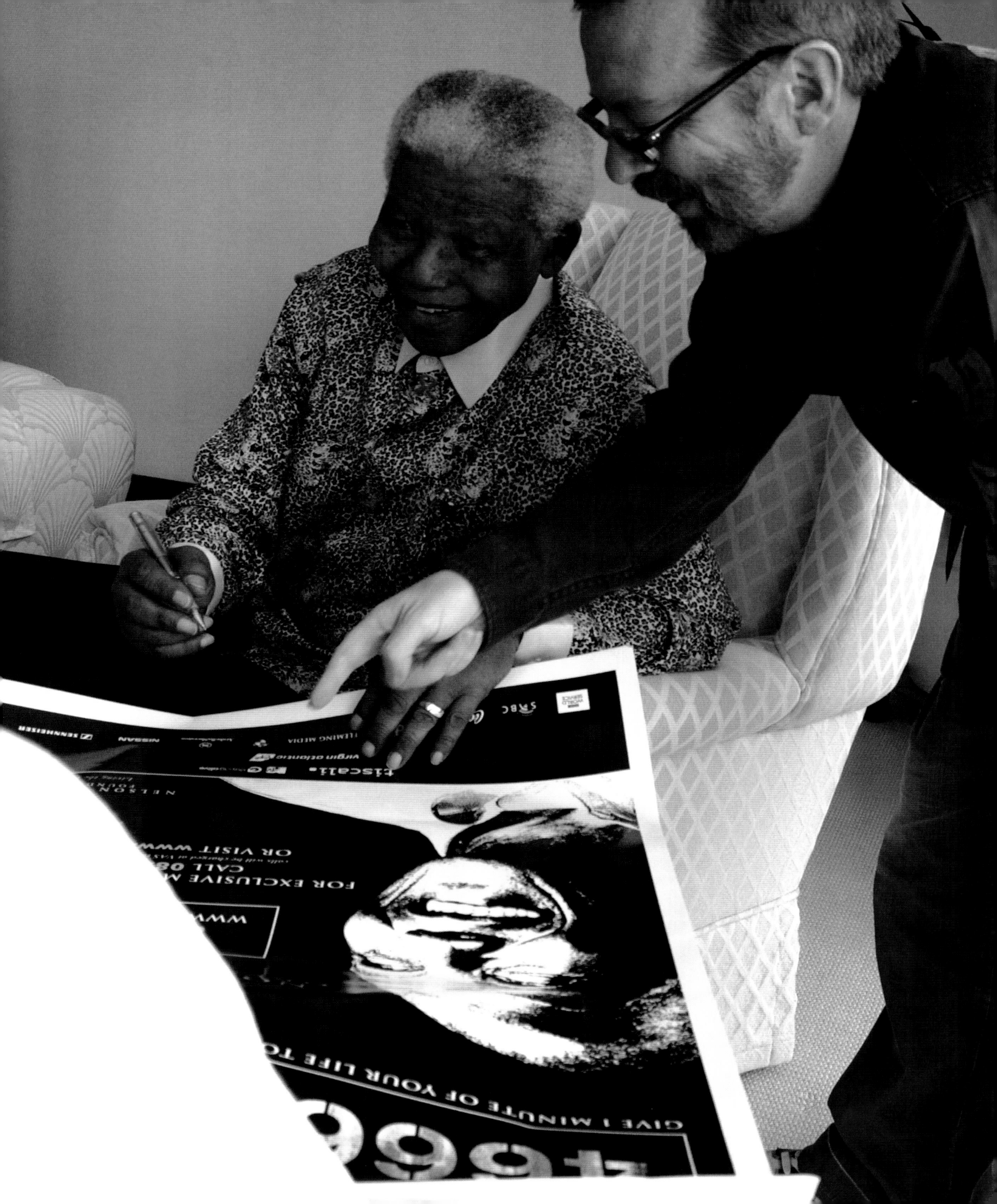
GIVE 1 MINUTE OF YOUR LIFE TO
FOR EXCLUSIVE
OR VISIT
tiscali
virgin atlantic
FLEMING MEDIA
NISSAN
SENNHEISER
SABC

"INSPIRED BY THE VISION AND LEADERSHIP OF NELSON MANDELA, THE 46664 CAMPAIGN AIMS TO RAISE AWARENESS OF THE GLOBAL HIV / AIDS PANDEMIC, AS WELL AS FUNDS FOR THE NELSON MANDELA FOUNDATION. THE FOUNDATION STRIVES TO REALISE THE IDEALS, GOALS AND VISION PURSUED BY MR MANDELA, IN PARTICULAR IN THE FIELD OF HIV / AIDS. THE PROCEEDS RAISED BY 46664 WILL GO TOWARDS IMPROVING THE LIVES OF THOSE INFECTED AND AFFECTED BY THE HIV / AIDS PANDEMIC, MOVING BEYOND AWARENESS-RAISING EXERCISES TOWARD DEVELOPING PARTNERSHIPS TO FACILITATE IMPLEMENTATION AND ACTION. RECOGNISING THAT AIDS IS MORE THAN JUST A DISEASE BUT A HUMAN RIGHTS ISSUE, THE MONEY WILL BE USED IN FOUR KEY AREAS: RESEARCH; TREATMENT, CARE AND SUPPORT; EDUCATION AND LEADERSHIP. IN PARTICULAR, THE PROCEEDS FROM THE 46664 CAMPAIGN WILL BE USED TO INITIATE, DEVELOP AND SUPPORT PRACTICAL PROGRAMMES FOR THE PREVENTION, TESTING, CARE AND SUPPORT FOR THOSE INFECTED AND AFFECTED BY HIV / AIDS."

JOHN SAMUEL, CHIEF EXECUTIVE OF THE NELSON MANDELA FOUNDATION.

TWENTY TWO

REHEARSALS

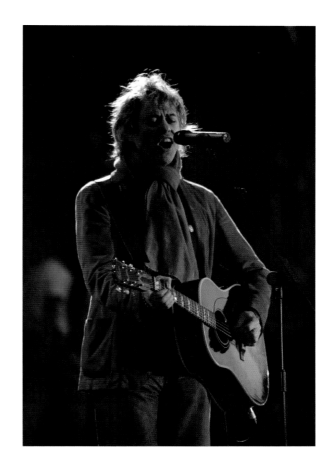

THE CONCERT

4666

crazy in love

crazy in love

BEYONCE

I hope to bring more awareness because, you know, I'm young and this is my first step in trying to make a change. And I've learned a lot of the myths and the rumours and the things that people believe here and some people just don't know. And I just want young people to know that the sexiest thing about being a woman is taking care of yourself. BEYONCE

BEING HERE IS ONE OF THE BEST DECISIONS I'VE EVER MADE IN MY LIFE. BEYONCE

I'M JUST HAPPY THAT HOPEFULLY I CAN BE A PART – WELL, I AM A PART OF SOMETHING THAT IS GOING TO HELP SO MANY PEOPLE. I FEEL LIKE CELEBRITIES HAVE A VOICE AND THEY CAN REACH PEOPLE THAT SOMETIMES POLITICIANS CAN'T REACH. AND THIS IS MY STEP TO TRY AND CHANGE SOMETHING.

BOB GELDOF

A man, Mandela, whose life can be characterised by the singular fight for justice through political action has come to the correct conclusion that AIDS is not a medical condition, it's a political one, and the only way that this scourge can be defeated is by concerted political action.

BOB GELDOF

REDEMPTION SONG

The condition is medical, the solution is political. BOB GELDOF

QUEEN

DAVID A STEWART

say it's not true

We're not politicians, we're just musicians using what we do as a platform to just raise awareness effectively. If you can get on TV in most countries worldwide, that's quite a good way of raising awareness. So this is really a way of pressurising politicians and pharmaceutical companies to make the drugs cheaply or freely available. ROGER TAYLOR

EN ÁFRICA HAY
11 MILLONES DE HUÉRFANOS
POR CAUSA DEL SIDA
QUE HA ELIMINADO A
GENERACIONES ENTERAS.

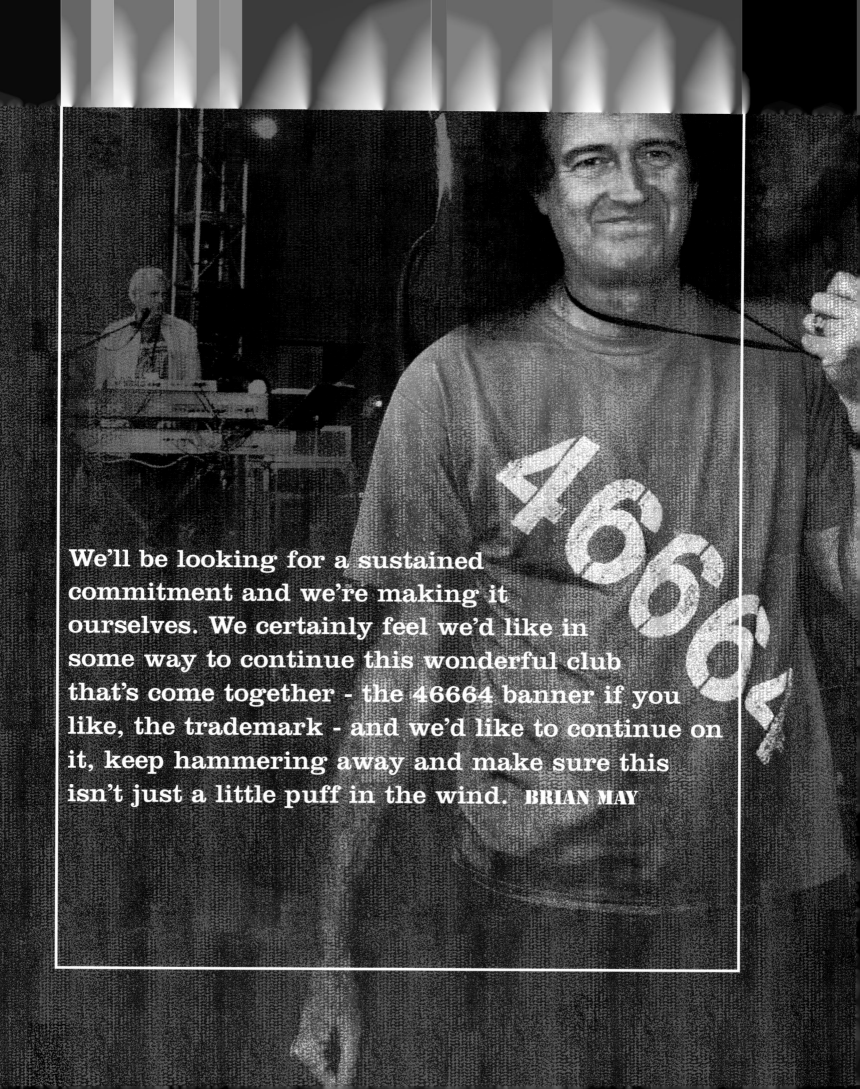

We'll be looking for a sustained commitment and we're making it ourselves. We certainly feel we'd like in some way to continue this wonderful club that's come together - the 46664 banner if you like, the trademark - and we'd like to continue on it, keep hammering away and make sure this isn't just a little puff in the wind. **BRIAN MAY**

PAUL OAKENFOLD /
SHIFTY SHELLSHOCK / TC

starry eyed surprise

WE FELT IT WAS REALLY IMPORTANT
TO COME DOWN AS A TEAM AND
PROMOTE THE EVENT AND WE'RE
ALSO USING SOME LOCAL TALENT -
SOME AFRICAN DRUMMERS AND AN
AFRICAN GUITARIST. I THOUGHT IT
WAS BETTER TO GET THE AFRICANS
INVOLVED BECAUSE OF WHAT IT
STANDS FOR. **PAUL OAKENFOLD**

BAABA MAAL
njilou

Le SIDA touche des personnes
de tous âges,
mais plus particulièrement
les jeunes

WE SEEM TO FORGET ALL THE ORPHANS WHO LOSE THEIR DAD AND MUM FROM THIS DISEASE. YOU KNOW THEY'RE GOING TO FACE A LOT OF THINGS WHICH ARE GOING TO BE VERY SAD FOR THEM. THEY'RE GOING TO FACE HAVING TO GROW UP WITH NO LOVE BECAUSE NO ONE CAN REPLACE MUM AND DAD. AT THE SAME TIME, IF WE DON'T TAKE CARE OF THEM... THEY'RE GOING TO NEED AN EDUCATION, THEY'RE GOING TO NEED TO UNDERSTAND, THEY'RE GOING TO NEED A PLACE IN SOCIETY, TO BE ACCEPTED AND SUPPORTED. **BAABA MAAL**

YOUSSOU N'DOUR
africa dream again

YUSUF ISLAM / PETER GABRIEL
wild world

I PARTICULARLY WANT TO CONTRIBUTE, IF YOU LIKE, THE CONCERN FOR PEOPLE'S SPIRITUALITY BECAUSE I THINK THAT LIFE ALSO REVOLVES AROUND HOW WE ARE INSIDE AND THAT INTERNAL SIDE HAS TO BE FIXED BEFORE YOU CAN FIX THE EXTERNAL. SO I BELIEVE THAT THAT'S MY MESSAGE TODAY. I'M SINGING A SONG CALLED WILD WORLD SO THE MESSAGE IS CLEAR. YUSUF ISLAM

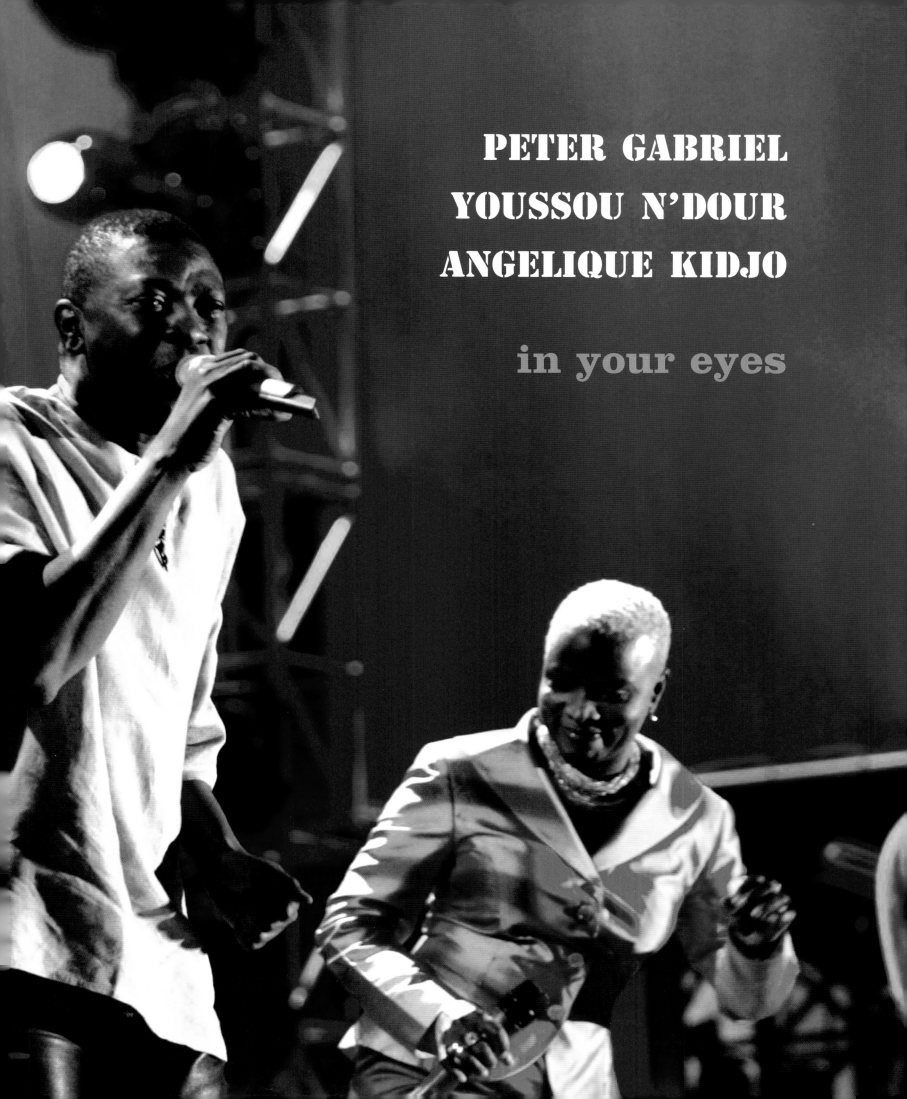

PETER GABRIEL
YOUSSOU N'DOUR
ANGELIQUE KIDJO

in your eyes

When you see images like Youssou N'Dour and
Peter Gabriel singing a great song, it's kind of
built something positive for Africa. Personally,
I'm really happy to play this song with Peter
here in Africa.   **YOUSSOU N'DOUR**

I WAS ALREADY INVOLVED IN WORKING WITH AIDS BEFORE I WAS CONTACTED TO DO THIS SHOW. AND OF COURSE, I SAID YES. FROM MEETINGS AND FINDING SOLUTIONS TO THE STAGE AND DOING WHAT I LOVE TO RAISE AWARENESS WORLDWIDE. WHAT'S BETTER THAN THAT? ANGELIQUE KIDJO

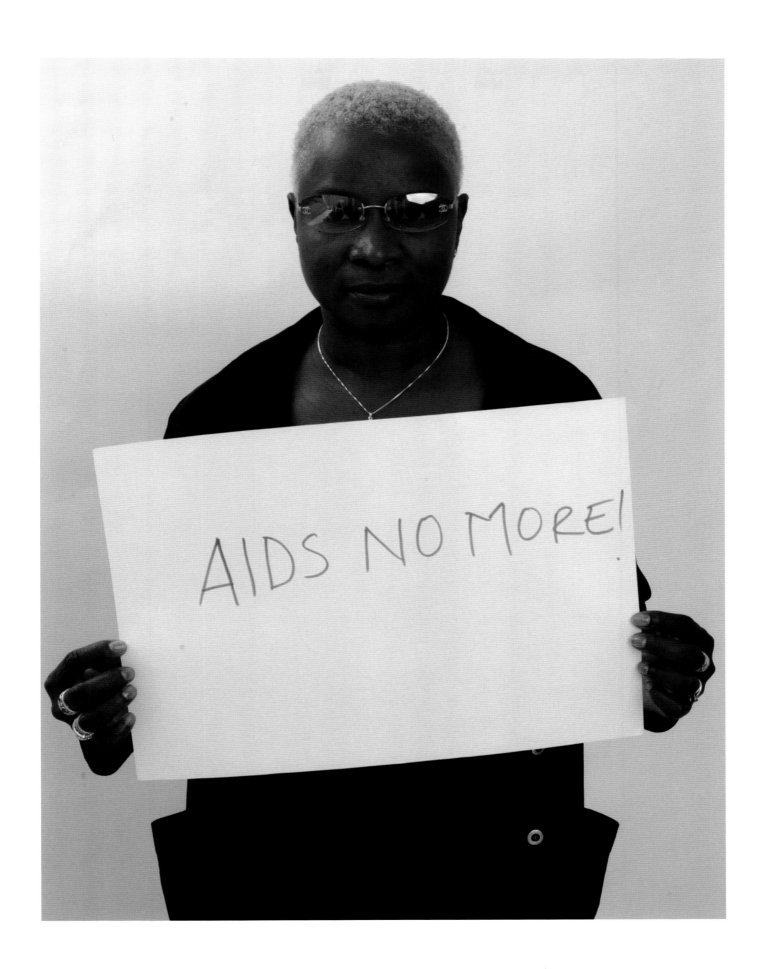

PETER GABRIEL
biko

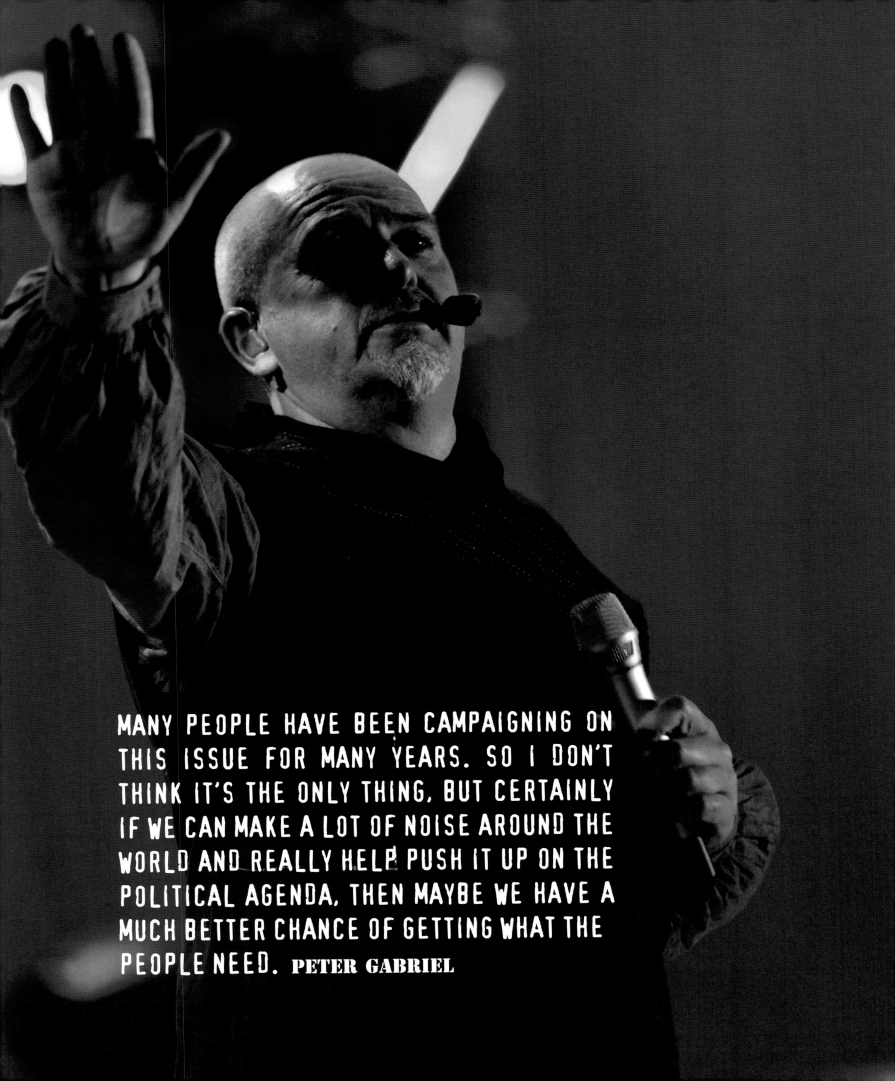

MANY PEOPLE HAVE BEEN CAMPAIGNING ON THIS ISSUE FOR MANY YEARS. SO I DON'T THINK IT'S THE ONLY THING, BUT CERTAINLY IF WE CAN MAKE A LOT OF NOISE AROUND THE WORLD AND REALLY HELP PUSH IT UP ON THE POLITICAL AGENDA, THEN MAYBE WE HAVE A MUCH BETTER CHANCE OF GETTING WHAT THE PEOPLE NEED. **PETER GABRIEL**

BONO

BEYONCE

THE EDGE

DAVID A STEWART

american prayer

NELSON MANDELA

QUEEN
invincible hope

ANGELIQUE KIDJO

afrika

The women are the spinebone of Africa but yet, the men don't give them the respect in the place they deserve. When you're married and your husband wants to have sex with you, it's not yours to say no. Even if your husband's doing something else, he's not meant to tell you. That is one of the problems. But the main problem is the education. If the mothers and women are educated, they can refuse to have sex with a man that doesn't want to protect himself.

ANGELIQUE KIDJO

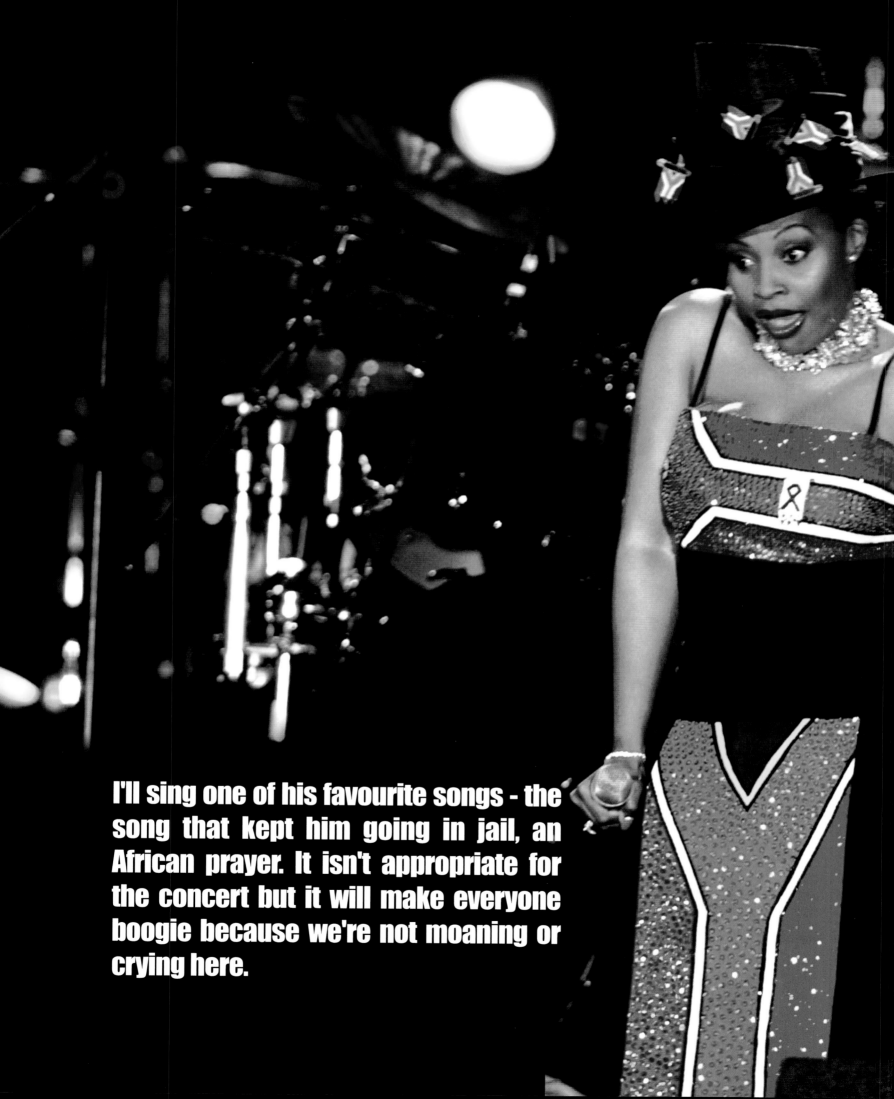

I'll sing one of his favourite songs - the song that kept him going in jail, an African prayer. It isn't appropriate for the concert but it will make everyone boogie because we're not moaning or crying here.

YVONNE CHAKA CHAKA
umqombothi

We're saying, "We want to make people happy and save lives, and collect money to save people's lives." That's how we'll do it. YVONNE CHAKA CHAKA

BONGO MAFFIN **the way**

NELSON MANDELA, YOU KNOW, MADE THE PEOPLE IN SOUTH AFRICA FREE. NOW IT'S TIME FOR US AND NELSON TO MAKE SURE THAT THE WORLD IS AIDS FREE.

BONGO MAFFIN

JOHNNY CLEGG AND GUESTS
asimbonanga

BECAUSE IT'S IN MY COUNTRY, IT'S MY EX-PRESIDENT, IT'S SOUTH AFRICANS WHO'VE COME AND SUPPORTED IT AND IT'S BEEN A TREMENDOUS HONOUR PARTICIPATING IN THIS AND IT'S A BIG HIGHLIGHT IN MY CAREER. JOHNNY CLEGG

PEOPLE
JOHNNY CLEGG / JIMMY CLIFF

PEOPLE

It's a global situation. AIDS is not limited to anyone so everyone wake up cos it could be you tomorrow. It could be your child or your grandchild so everyone wake up now and just do your part. JIMMY CLIFF

ESS

THE CORRS

breathless

NORMALLY, YOU DO A SHOW AND JUST DO WHAT YOU DO BUT IN THIS WAY WE'RE DOING THINGS WITH OTHER ARTISTS WHICH MAKES IT REALLY INTERESTING FOR US AND VERY MUSICALLY INSPIRATIONAL FOR US. CAROLINE CORR

IT'S SYMBOLIC THAT THERE'S A LOT OF PEOPLE MIXING ON THE STAGE AND COMING TOGETHER COS THAT'S WHAT THE WORLD HAS TO DO TO FIGHT THIS HUGE CRISIS. **JIM CORR**

LADYSMITH BLACK MAMBAZO / THE CORRS
leliungelo elakho

LADYSMITH BLACK MAMBAZO
homeless

ANDREA CORR
BRIAN MAY
is this the world
we created?

ABDEL WRIGHT
loose we now

HONESTLY, I HOPE PEOPLE DON'T LOOK ON THE SHOW AS LIKE, "OH, BEYONCE'S PERFORMING! OH, BONO!" YOU KNOW, THAT HYPE. I HOPE THEY GET THE MESSAGE THESE WONDERFUL ARTISTS ARE CARRYING. BECAUSE YOU'LL ALWAYS SEE BONO AND BEYONCE PERFORM AS LONG AS WE LIVE BUT THIS MESSAGE PARTICULARLY TONIGHT IT'S VERY IMPORTANT. WE NEED TO GET THE GRIP OF IT.

ABDEL WRIGHT

DANNY K

hurts so bad

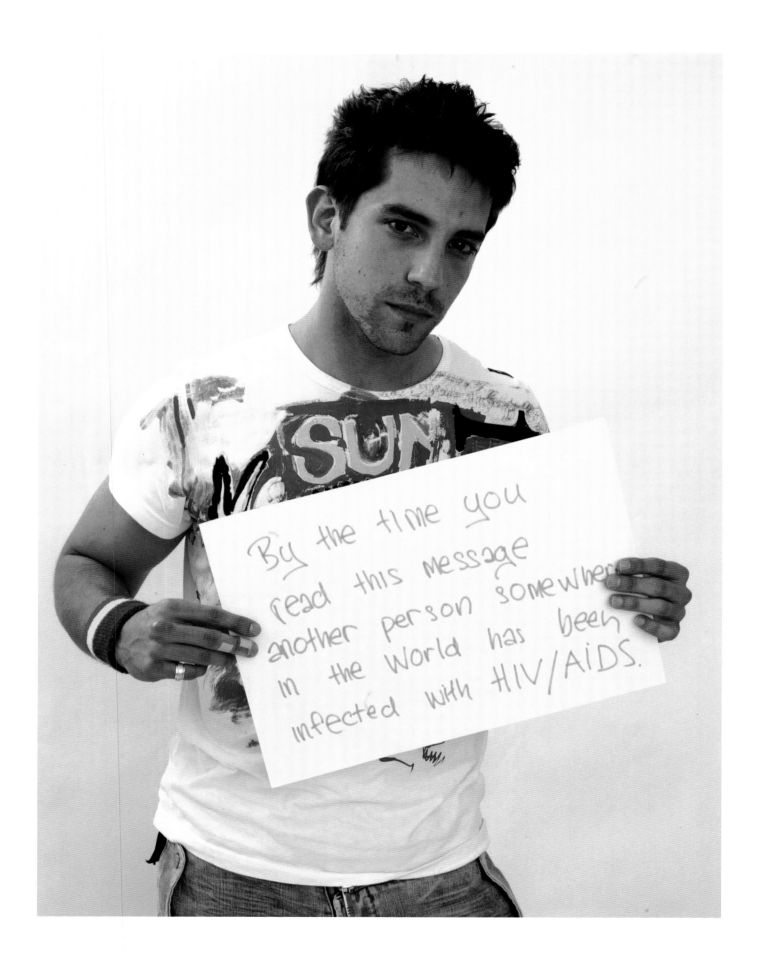

I WAS GIVEN THE ENORMOUS HONOUR OF BEING INVITED ON THIS BILL. IT WAS A DECISION I MADE IN ABOUT .3 OF A SECOND. I SAID, "ABSOLUTELY." IT'S A GREAT PRIVILEGE FOR ME AS A YOUNG SOUTH AFRICAN ARTIST TO SHARE THE STAGE WITH MY FELLOW COUNTRYMEN AND SOME GREAT INTERNATIONAL PEOPLE TOO. DANNY K

WATERSHED
indigo girl

IT'S A NICE STEPPING STONE AND A GREAT START TO SOMETHING THAT IS HOPEFULLY GOING TO DO THE WORLD A WORLD OF GOOD. **WATERSHED**

THE GREAT SONG OF

INDIFFERENCE

(WHAT'S SO FUNNY 'BOUT)

PEACE LOVE

AND UNDERSTANDING

BOB GELDOF

ZUCCHERO / QUEEN / SHARON CORR

everybody's got to learn sometime

We can be together and do more of these things.
The message will arrive one day loud and clear.

ZUCCHERO

EL SIDA YA NO ES SÓLO UNA ENFERMEDAD: SE HA CONVERTIDO EN UNA CUESTIÓN DE DERECHOS HUMANOS.

EURYTHMICS
here comes the rain again

WHEN FREEDOM RISES *46664
FROM THE KILLING FLOOR
NO LOCK OF IRON OR RIVET
CAN RESTRAIN THE DOOR
AND NO KIND OF ARMY
CAN HOPE TO WIN A WAR
LIKE TRYING TO STOP THE RAIN
OR STILL THE LION'S ROAR

LIKE TRYING TO STOP THE WHIRLWIND
SCATTERING SEEDS AND SPORE
LIKE TRYING TO STOP THE TIN CANS RAPPING OU
JAILHOUSE SEMAPHORE

THEY KNOW █████ WHEN YOUR HANDS ARE MANACLED
IT'S YOUR SPIRIT THAT GETS RAW
BUT NOT THAT THE SMALLER PATCH OF SKY YOU SEE
THE MORE YOUR VISIONS SOAR

IN THE GHETTOS OF THE COLOURS
DON'T FORGET THE HUMAN CORE
IN THE TOWNSHIPS OF HUMANITY
THERE WOULD BE NO POOR
FROM WHERE THE ROCK IS HEAVY
COMES THE PUREST ORE
THE FIRST SIX WAVES MIGHT BREAK IN THE BAY
BUT THE SEVENTH BREAKS ON THE SHORE

THE FACT THAT NELSON MANDELA WANTED TO USE HIS PRISON NUMBER 46664 AS A SYMBOL OF HOPE, USING WHAT MUST HAVE BEEN SUCH A PAINFUL SYMBOL FOR HIM, AND TURNING IT FROM NEGATIVE ENERGY INTO POSITIVE ENERGY, IS THE REASON HE IS SUCH A GREAT SPOKESPERSON IN THE STRUGGLE FOR A HUMANE AND JUST WORLD.

IT'S ALSO WHY HE'S THE WORLD'S MOST RESPECTED AND TRUSTED LEADER IN THE GLOBAL FIGHT AGAINST AIDS.

WHEN I TALKED TO THE LATE JOE STRUMMER ABOUT WRITING A SONG LYRIC USING THIS NUMBER -- 46664 - AS A SONG OF HOPE, IT WAS LIKE GIVING THE CAPTAIN OF A RENEGADE ARMY THE GREEN LIGHT TO LIBERATE THE TOWN.

JOE'S LYRICS CAME OUT OF MY FAX MACHINE AS IF THEY WERE INSTRUCTIONS FOR A SECRET RENDEZVOUS WRITTEN BY A REBEL SOLDIER IN THE TRENCHES.

WHEN BONO AND I RECORDED THE TRACK, BONO STARTED SPONTANEOUSLY SINGING 'IT'S A LONG WALK TO FREEDOM,' TIPPING HIS HAT TO NELSON MANDELA'S BIOGRAPHY. IT GAVE THE SONG EVEN MORE RESONANCE AND MEANING.

AT THE END OF THE SESSION, WE ALL TALKED ABOUT JOE, HOW GREAT HE WAS, AND HOW HIS WORDS FOR THE SONG WERE SO STRONG AND HEARTFELT, AND ONES THAT WE WILL ALWAYS CHERISH. **DAVE STEWART**

For me it's the first time I've been in a free South Africa. It's early days, I know, ten years into democracy is just a blonk in the grand scale of things. But to be here knowing there is a future, it's really satisfying. In fact, I almost can't express how moved I am. **ANNIE LENNOX**

EURYTHMICS
YOUSSOU N'DOUR
seven seconds

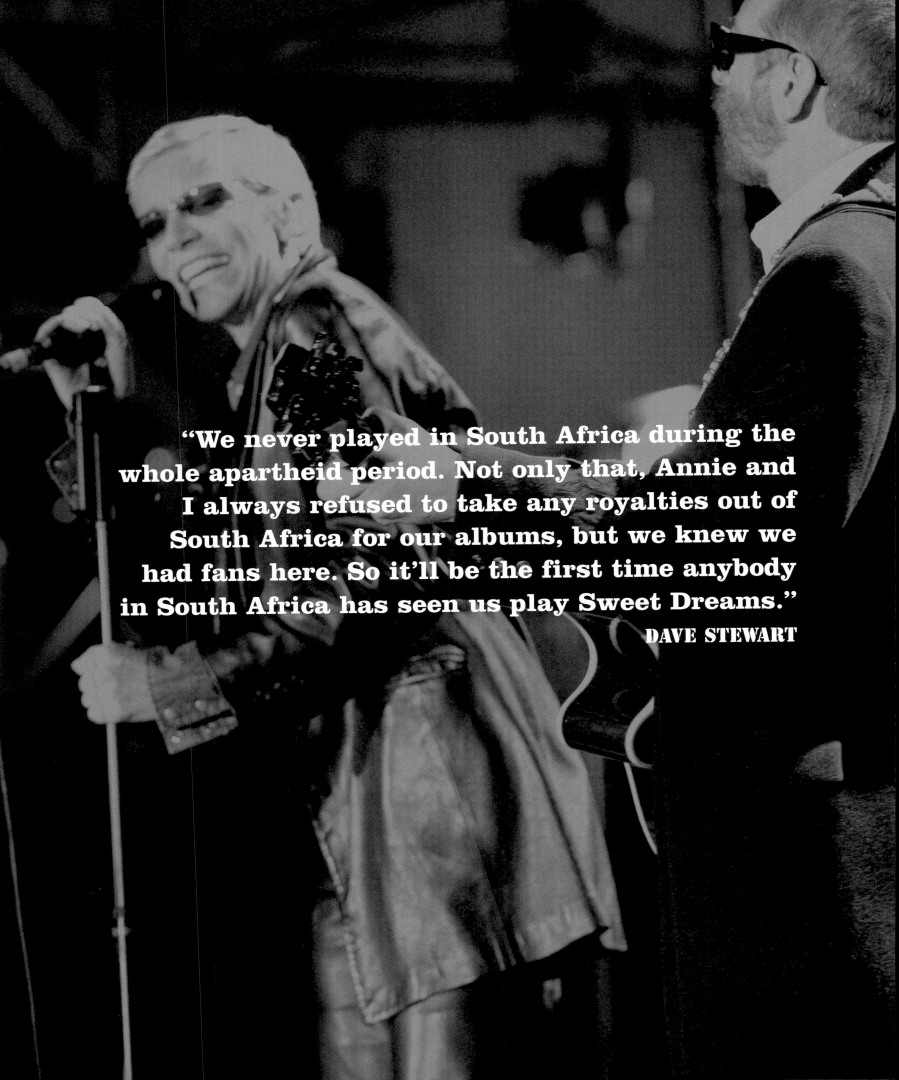

"We never played in South Africa during the whole apartheid period. Not only that, Annie and I always refused to take any royalties out of South Africa for our albums, but we knew we had fans here. So it'll be the first time anybody in South Africa has seen us play Sweet Dreams."

DAVE STEWART

EURYTHMICS
sweet dreams (are made of this)

MS DYNAMITE
don't throw your life away

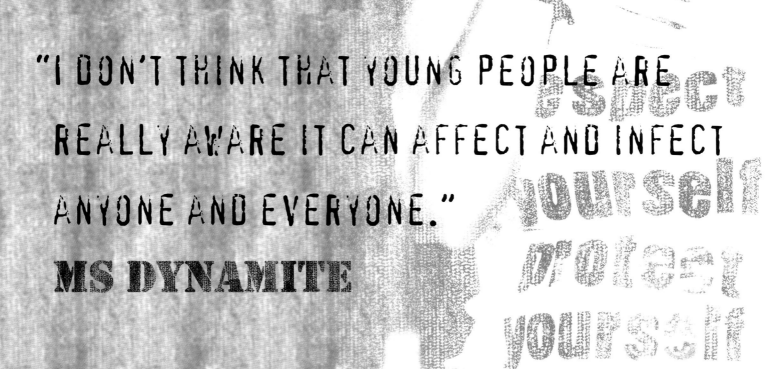

"I DON'T THINK THAT YOUNG PEOPLE ARE REALLY AWARE IT CAN AFFECT AND INFECT ANYONE AND EVERYONE."
MS DYNAMITE

THERE'S SO MANY ELEMENTS TO IT THAT ARE SO AMAZING. ALL THE ARTISTS COMING TOGETHER, THE CAUSE, NELSON MANDELA... THERE'S JUST SO MANY FACTORS AND I'M DEFINITELY HONOURED TO BE A PART OF IT.

I THINK I'D SAY TO YOUNG PEOPLE SIMPLY TO PROTECT YOURSELF AT ALL TIMES. AIDS IS NOT SOMETHING THAT DISCRIMINATES AGAINST PARTICULAR SETS OF PEOPLE - RICH, POOR, YOUNG, OLD, BLACK, WHITE, GAY, STRAIGHT. IT AFFECTS EVERYONE, EVERY DAY, EVERYWHERE.

MS DYNAMITE

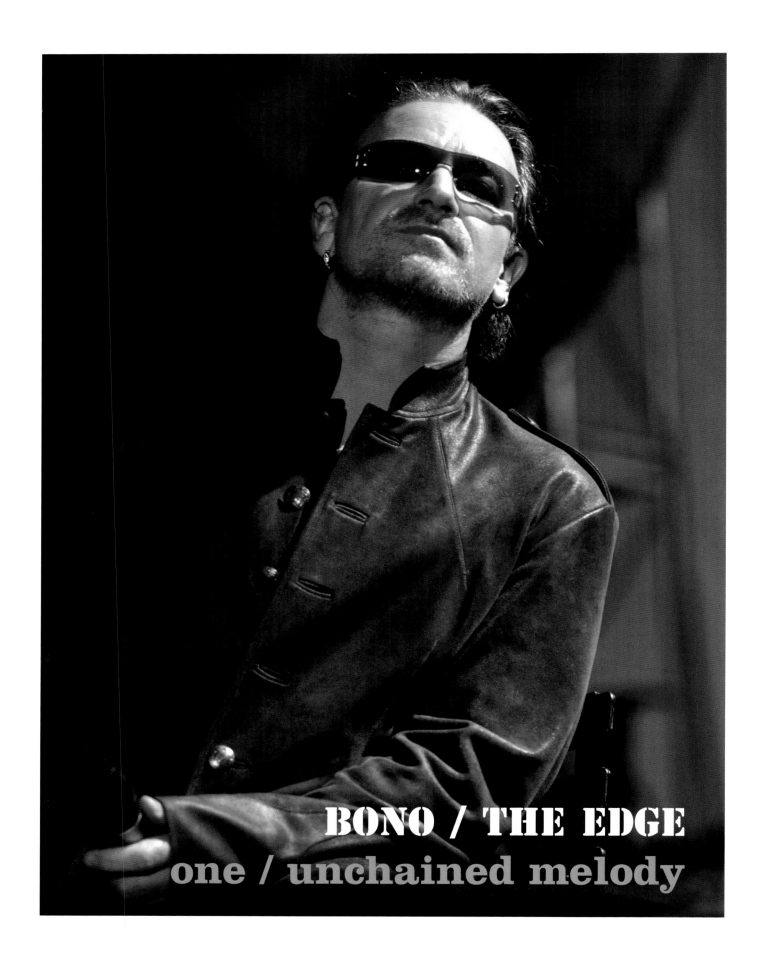

BONO / THE EDGE
one / unchained melody

MAKE A LOT OF FUSS. THIS IS AN EMERGENCY. MAKE A LOT OF FUSS. EVERYONE CAN HELP, EVERYONE HAS A PART TO PLAY IN DRAWING ATTENTION TO THIS PROBLEM. AND HIV AIDS, THERE SHOULD BE NO STIGMA. IT'S A MEDICAL PROBLEM, IT'S NOTHING MORE THAN THAT. AND WE HAVE THE RESOURCES AND THE TOOLS TO SORT IT OUT BUT WE JUST NEED THE WILL.

THE EDGE

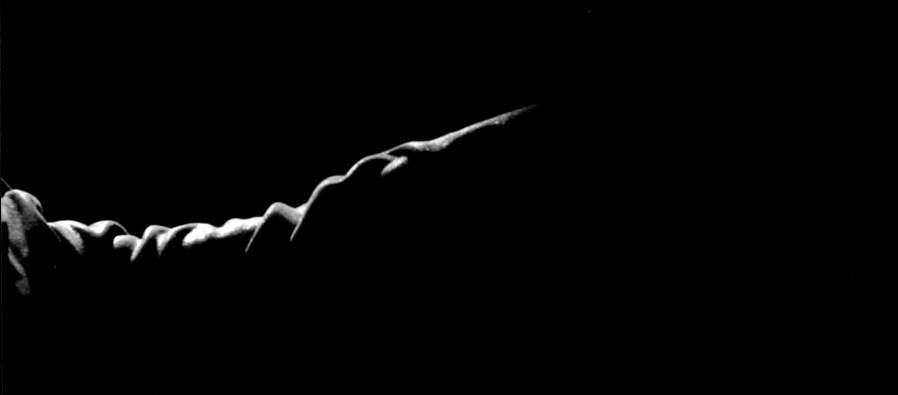

BONO / QUEEN / ANASTACIA
DAVE STEWART
AND ANDREWS BONSU

amandla

AS DEEP AS ALL OF OUR POCKETS ARE HERE BEING RICH, SPOILED-ROTTEN ROCK STARS WE CANNOT AFFORD TO FIX THIS PROBLEM NO MATTER HOW MUCH WE GIVE. IT'S GOING TO TAKE GOVERNMENTS. IT'S GOING TO TAKE LEADERSHIP FROM TONY BLAIR, FROM BUSH. IT'S JUST GOING TO TAKE LEADERSHIP FROM THE WORLD. **BONO**

I am Andrews Bonsu and I'm speaking for the future of Africa. Please help us to save my continent and help us to save my brothers and sisters infected with HIV/AIDS. And I want to tell you that you should give one minute of your life to stop AIDS now. **ANDREWS BONSU**

QUEEN
ZUCCHERO
THANDISWA MAZWAI

MEDLEY –
BOHEMIAN RHAPSODY, I WANT IT ALL, I WANT TO BREAK FREE, RADIO GAGA

QUEEN / ANASTACIA /
AMAMPONDO DRUMMERS
we will rock you

KNOWING BEYONCE AND MS. DYNAMITE, I KNOW THEIR TENACITY IS THE SAME AS MINE, WE'RE NOT GOING TO STOP FOR ANY CAUSE, WE'RE GOING TO KEEP ON GOING AND KEEP ON BEING VERY OUTSPOKEN AS WOMEN.

ANASTACIA

QUEEN / ANASTACIA / CAST
we are the champions

MORE THAN A DECADE AGO, NELSON MANDELA LED THE WORLD IN A TRIUMPHANT FIGHT AGAINST APARTHEID. NOW HE HAS STEPPED FORWARD TO LEAD US IN THE FIGHT AGAINST AIDS. IT IS FITTING THAT THE GREATEST LEADER OF OUR TIME HAS CHOSEN TO FIGHT AIDS AS HIS FINAL CHALLENGE. AIDS IS NO MERE DISEASE. IT IS THE GREATEST DISASTER IN HUMAN HISTORY. IT THREATENS OUR MOST BASIC HUMAN RIGHTS, OUR HUMANITY AND OUR COMMON FUTURE.

PRESIDENT MANDELA'S VISION IS THAT EVERY SINGLE ONE OF US, EVERYWHERE IN THE WORLD, STANDS UP TO AIDS. 46664 IS A SYMBOL OF THAT SOLIDARITY. IT IS A CAMPAIGN TO CHANGE THE WORLD, TO MAKE THIS A WORLD IN WHICH 9,000 PEOPLE WILL NOT DIE NEEDLESSLY TODAY AND EVERY DAY OF A DISEASE THAT WE KNOW HOW TO BEAT. WE HAVE AT OUR DISPOSAL EFFECTIVE TOOLS THAT CAN SAVE MILLIONS OF LIVES. EVERY INFECTION CAN BE PREVENTED. EVERY CASE CAN BE TREATED.

IN NOVEMBER 2003, AN EXTRAORDINARY LINE-UP OF PERFORMERS ANSWERED PRESIDENT MANDELA'S CALL BY COMING TO CAPE TOWN AND, THROUGH ONE OF THE GREATEST CHARITY CONCERTS EVER, BRING HIS MESSAGE ON AIDS TO MILLIONS OF VIEWERS ALLOVER THE WORLD. THROUGH THEIR MUSIC AND THEIR WORDS, THEY SPREAD A MESSAGE OF HOPE AND OF COMMITMENT: YOU AND I – EVERY ONE OF US – CAN DO OUR PART TO STOP THE SPREAD OF AIDS.

IN JULY 2004, AT THE 15TH INTERNATIONAL AIDS CONFERENCE IN BANGKOK, PRESIDENT MANDELA REITERATED HIS CALL TO ACTION BY ALL, AND HE IN PARTICULAR CALLED ON THE WORLD'S LEADERS TO REDUCE STIGMA, RESPECT HUMAN RIGHTS AND INCREASE FUNDING FOR THIS GLOBAL FIGHT.

IN THIS BIG FIGHT, THE GLOBAL FUND'S ROLE IS TO GET RESOURCES FROM THOSE THAT CAN AFFORD IT—GOVERNMENTS, BUSINESSES, INDIVIDUALS—TO THOSE WHO CAN USE THEM BEST. SO FAR, MORE THAN 300 PROGRAMS IN NEARLY 130 COUNTRIES ARE BEING SUPPORTED. MILLIONS OF COMMITTED PEOPLE IN BOTH PUBLIC AND FAITH-BASED HEALTH SERVICES, IN NON-GOVERNMENTAL ORGANIZATIONS, IN PRIVATE CORPORATIONS AND IN THE MEDIA, BATTLE ON THE FRONTLINES WITH FINANCIAL BACKING FROM THE GLOBAL FUND. IN THE YEARS TO COME, THE GLOBAL FUND WILL CONTINUE TO INCREASE ITS FUNDING TO HUNDREDS MORE PROGRAMS, ALLOWING THOSE ON THE FRONT LINES TO DESIGN THE MOST EFFECTIVE ACTIVITIES FOR THEIR COUNTRY AND COMMUNITY.

BUT MONEY ALONE IS NOT ENOUGH. YOUR ACTIONS ARE THE BASIS OF TRUE CHANGE. PRACTICE SAFE SEX. PUT AN END TO STIGMA. VOLUNTEER YOUR TIME AND YOUR SKILL. GIVE ONE MINUTE OF YOUR LIFE TO AIDS – OR ONE WEEK OR ONE YEAR. RISE UP, ROLL UP YOUR SLEEVES AND PITCH IN. PRESIDENT MANDELA'S APPEAL IS A CALL TO SERVICE. LET'S ANSWER IT TOGETHER AND CREATE A WORLD FREE FROM AIDS.

PROFESSOR RICHARD G. A. FEACHEM
EXECUTIVE DIRECTOR
THE GLOBAL FUND TO FIGHT AIDS, TUBERCULOSIS AND MALARIA.

46664

Abdel Wright	**Jimmy Cliff**
Amampondo Drummers	**Johnny Clegg**
Anastacia	**Ladysmith Black Mambazo**
Andrews Bonsu	**Ms Dynamite**
Angelique Kidjo	**Paul Oakenfold**
Baaba Maal	**Peter Gabriel**
Beyoncé	**Queen**
Bob Geldof	**Shifty Shellshock**
Bongo Maffin	**TC**
Bono	**Watershed**
The Corrs	**Youssou N'Dour**
Danny K	**Yusuf Islam**
The Edge	**Yvonne Chaka Chaka.**
Eurythmics	**Zucchero**

House Band: Spike Edney – Musical Director, Keyboards, Vocals. Jamie Moses – Guitar, Vocals. Eric Singer – Drums. Treana Morris – Backing Vocals. Chris Thompson – Backing Vocals. Zoe Nicholas – Backing Vocals. Mandisa Dlanga – Backing Vocals. Bongani Masuka – Backing Vocals. Jeff Leach – Programmer, Keyboards. Paul Weimar – Alto Sax, Flute. Steve Stroud – Bass, Vocals. Spencer Mbadu – Bass. Mike Kearsay – Trombone. Andy Bush – Trumpet, Flugelhorn. Keith Prior – Drums, Percussion. Steve Hamilton – Tenor Sax, Flute. Frank Paco – Drums. Antonio Paco – Percussion. Stanislav Anguelov – Accordion.

A Big Thank You to the "Heavenly" Soweto Gospel Choir.

46664 Inspired by Nelson Mandela and carried forward by David A Stewart

Artistic and Music Directors: Brian May, David A Stewart & Roger Taylor

Produced by Jim Beach and JF Cecillon

Photography by Richard Young, Dave Benett, Frank Micelotta, Dave Hogan

Art Direction David Costa

Book Design: Emil Dacany, Nadine Levy and Sian Rance for Wherefore Art?

Event Financing By Fleming Media LLP
Financial Management JP Sacau

Event Marketing: The Music Matrix Ltd
General Event Management: Tim Massey
Artist Liaison: Lizzie Anders
Event Production: Robbie Williams, Nick Levitt, Liz Holden, Helen Campbell, Steve Jones for RW Productions
Set Design: Mark Fisher, Ray Winkler
Lighting Designer: Bruce Ramus
Event Promoter: Roddy Quinn for Real Concerts
46664.com: Anthony Cauchi, Nick Weymouth for Outside Line
Publicity and PR: Shimon Cohen for The PR Office, Phil Symes for The PR Contact
Legal: Lee & Thompson and Addleshaw Goddard

46664 The Concert

Directed by David Mallet
TV Executive Producers: Malcolm Gerrie, Andy Ward, Frances Naylor.
TV Program Producer: Lisa Chapman
Filmed by Initial Television
Recorded by Justin Shirley Smith, Tim Summerhayes, Toby Allington
Mixed by David Richards and Joshua J Macrae at Mountain Studios (Montreux, Switzerland) and The Priory (Surrey, UK).
Mastered by David Richards at Mountain Studios and Tim Young and Twig at Metropolis Mastering.
DVD Associate Producer: Simon Lupton

CD Part 1 – "African Prayer"   CD Part 2 – "Long Walk to Freedom",   CD Part 3 – "Amandla"

DVD "46664 – The Event"

Very special thanks to Jakes Gerwal, John Samuel, Iqbal Meer, Anant Singh, Zelda La Grange, Maeline Engelbrecht, Dr. Connie Kganakga and everyone at The Nelson Mandela Foundation and to Sir Richard Branson.

Special thanks to Tiscali, Vodafone, MTV Staying Alive, Virgin Atlantic, DATA, SABC, BBC World Service, The Global Fund, FedEx, Coca-Cola, The Mercury Phoenix Trust, Sennheiser, Sheraton Hotels, Sun International, BMW, Nissan, Motorola, Warner Music for their support.

And last but certainly not least, a massive thank you to all of the artists, their management teams and all the people involved who worked so hard to launch 46664.

To Madiba. "AIDS is no longer just a disease, it is a human rights issue"